DATE DUE

Chris Burke

He Overcame Down Syndrome

Gregory Lee

illustrated by Glenn Davis

The Rourke Corporation, Inc. Vero Beach, Florida

The Rourke Corporation, Inc.
P.O. Box 3328, Vero Beach, FL 32964

Series Editor: Gregory Lee
Production: The Creative Spark, San Clemente, CA

Library of Congress Cataloging-in-Publication Data

Lee, Gregory, 1956-
    Chris Burke: he overcame Down syndrome / by Gregory Lee.
        p. cm. — (Reaching your goal)
    Summary: Describes the life of a young man with Down syndrome who fulfilled his dream of becoming a television star.
    ISBN 0-86593-263-8
    1. Burke, Chris, 1965- . 2. Down's syndrome—Patients—United States—Biography—Juvenile literature. 3. Success—Juvenile literature. [1. Burke, Chris, 1965- . 2. Actors and actresses. 3. Down's syndrome. 4. Mentally handicapped.]
I. Title. II. Series.
RC571.B88L44 1993
362.1'96858842'0092—dc20
[B]   93-18213
                                        CIP
                                        AC

"I'm going to be an actor," said Chris Burke.
No one believed him. His family and friends
knew that Chris would probably not become an
actor. He had Down syndrome.

Years ago people with Down syndrome were
treated as helpless and "retarded." No one
believed they could be normal. Today this
syndrome is better understood. People with
Down syndrome can do almost everything you
can do.

Chris Burke was born in New York City on August 26, 1965. His parents were named Frank and Marian. Chris's family always gave him lots of love. They wanted him to have an ordinary childhood.

Chris went to a special school when he was young. His classmates had Down syndrome, too. They learned and played games.

Chris liked to watch TV. He wanted to be an actor ever since he was nine years old. He loved to make up little plays in school that he performed for his friends and teachers.

Some adults told Chris's parents that he would never be a "normal child." But Frank and Marian ignored them. They made sure he had new clothes to wear, just like other children. They made him behave, just like their other children.

Frank and Marian Burke believed their son could have a happy life with or without Down syndrome.

When Chris was older, he went to a boarding school in Massachusetts where he lived with other boys. The school had a farm where the children could learn about animals. Down syndrome did not keep Chris from enjoying life.

Chris became a Boy Scout. Twice he helped other boys who had been hurt outdoors. Chris was not helpless.

Chris enjoyed trying out for sports. He played soccer and baseball and basketball. "He was a spunky little athlete," said his coach. When he was nine, he was in the broad jump in the Special Olympics.

In his teens, he began writing stories and ideas for TV shows. He wrote long letters to his favorite stars. He told everyone he met that someday he was going to be a movie star.

His mother said, "I don't think it's good for him to have such goals because he'll never make it." His brother and two sisters felt the same way.

Chris was not upset with his "handicap." He often said he had "Up syndrome." So he kept his dream of becoming an actor.

Chris never missed his favorite shows and music videos. He taped dozens of movies and knew the lines by heart. His family thought this was a waste of time.

Finding a job for people with Down syndrome isn't easy. Chris's family knew he would have to search hard to find one.

When Chris left school he got a job at Public School 138. He ran an elevator. His parents were glad. This was a good job for Chris. But Chris also went to a night school for adults like himself to learn acting.

One day Chris's friend heard about a part in a TV movie. An actor with Down syndrome was needed! The friend told the TV people all about Chris. Chris tried out for the part.

His dad took him to the audition. Chris was excited and confident. He got the part. Chris jumped and yelled with delight.

Chris was on a movie set at last. He loved working with real actors. He got their autographs. At last his dream was coming true.

His parents told him not to get his hopes up. They said the movie was a once-in-a-lifetime moment. Chris should not expect to act again.

When the movie was finally broadcast, Chris's family gathered about the TV to watch him act. Millions of other people saw Chris, too.

The movie did so well that the network wanted to make up a whole TV series about a character with Down syndrome. It was called *Life Goes On*.

No one with Down syndrome had ever starred in a weekly TV show. But Chris Burke did it. The show stayed on the air for several years. Chris receives lots of fan mail from others with Down syndrome. They say he inspires them.

"There's one thing I don't like," says Chris Burke. "That's when people say that we are 'victims' of Down syndrome. Down syndrome isn't a disease. I was born with Down syndrome. Everybody is born different. This is just who I am."

"Maybe someday they'll just describe me as 'Chris Burke, the actor.'"

Working on a TV show is not easy. It's hard work. Chris has to work extra hard because he gets tired. His fellow actors are amazed at Chris. They say he is a good actor.

Chris kept a list of goals when he was young. One of his goals was to become an actor by age 23. He became one at 21.

Christopher Burke now has a school named after him. Handicapped children love it when Chris visits the school. He always makes time for children.

Reaching Your Goal

What do you want to do? Do you want to be an astronaut? A cook? If you want something you must first set goals. Here are some steps to help you reach them.

1. Explore Your Goals

Asking questions can help you decide if reaching your goal is what you really want.

Will I be happier if I reach this goal?
Will I be healthier if I reach this goal?

2. Name Your Goals

It is harder to choose a goal if it is too general. Do you want to be "happy?"

Learn to blow up a balloon.
Learn to ride a two-wheel bicycle.
Finish a book a week.

Name the goals you want to reach.

3. Start Small
Try reaching your goal with smaller goals.
Do you want to learn to skateboard?
Try standing on it first without moving.
Do you want to build a dollhouse?
Have an adult show you how to use tools.

4. Small Goals Turn Into Big Ones
Learning to improve your spelling can be
a goal.
Practice shorter words first.
Learn to use bigger words in sentences.
Enter a spelling bee.

5. Stick With It
People like Chris Burke reached their goals by
working hard. They didn't let others talk them
out of their goals. You can do it too!

Reaching Your Goal Books

Jim Abbott Left-handed Wonder

Hans Christian Andersen A Fairy Tale Life

Cher Singer and Actress

Chris Burke He Overcame Down Syndrome

Henry Cisneros A Hard Working Mayor

Beverly Cleary She Makes Reading Fun

Bill Cosby Superstar

Roald Dahl Kids Love His Stories

Jane Goodall The Chimpanzee's Friend

Jim Henson Creator of the Muppets

Jesse Jackson A Rainbow Leader

Michael Jordan A Team Player

Ted Kennedy, Jr. A Lifetime of Challenges

Jackie Joyner-Kersee Track-and-Field Star

Ray Kroc Famous Restaurant Owner

Christa McAuliffe Reaching for the Stars

Dale Murphy Baseball's Gentle Giant

Arnold Schwarzenegger Hard Work Brought Success

Dr. Seuss We Love You

Charles Schulz Great Cartoonist

Samantha Smith Young Ambassador

Steven Spielberg He Makes Great Movies

Rourke Corporation, Inc.
P.O. Box 3328
Vero Beach, FL 32964